GW00835964

ABANDONED
IOWA
VACANT HEARTLAND

MITCH NICHOLSON

AMERICA
THROUGH TIME®
ADDING COLOR TO AMERICAN HISTORY

America Through Time is an imprint of Fonthill Media LLC
www.through-time.com
office@through-time.com

Published by Arcadia Publishing by arrangement with Fonthill Media LLC
For all general information, please contact Arcadia Publishing:
Telephone: 843-853-2070
Fax: 843-853-0044
E-mail: sales@arcadiapublishing.com
For customer service and orders:
Toll-Free 1-888-313-2665

www.arcadiapublishing.com

First published 2020

Copyright © Mitch Nicholson 2020

ISBN 978-1-63499-235-0

All rights reserved. No part of this publication may be reproduced, stored in a retrieval
system or transmitted in any form or by any means, electronic, mechanical, photocopying,
recording or otherwise, without prior permission in writing from Fonthill Media LLC

Typeset in Trade Gothic 10pt on 15pt
Printed and bound in England

CONTENTS

ACKNOWLEDGMENTS

I must start by acknowledging my partner on the road, local photographer, equestrian artist, and dearest friend, Lisa. This project would have died if not for her creative input and perspective. Lisa has been a constant source of inspiration and motivation since the early days of *Abandoned Iowa*.

Next, heartfelt thanks to my family for the constant support and encouragement. Without their support, I would have never owned the camera I first picked up to start the project, nor would I have been pushed to keep pursuing my passion.

PREFACE

Abandonments carry decades of their own experience. A constant theme of my work is the treatment of the structures—be it a school, bridge, or hospital—as a character, not a setting. In my write-ups about the locations I visit, unlike in this preface, I refuse to use first-person verbiage. The words "I," "my," or "me" detract from the content, and character, of the location or structure.

History and emotional connections are revealed from commenting visitors to my pages. Someone may have experienced great happiness and joy in the classroom of a now dilapidated school, or conversely, great sadness upon seeing the current state of an abandoned structure. My role is to capture, document, and present the structures as they are—regardless of their future.

Conversations of renovation, urges to restore, and promotion of preservation efforts are frequent on my page, given the historical value and significance of some the structures I visit. It is my position to remain neutral in these conversations and simply document and present the structures as they are. Keeping my thoughts and impressions out of the conversation allows the viewer to draw their own conclusions and experience the location for themselves.

The first location: a dirt road leading to a non-existent bridge.

INTRODUCTION

I started the ongoing photo-journalistic project known as "Abandoned Iowa" in the fall of 2010, after getting off to a difficult start as an English undergraduate at a small private college. At the time, I thought I wanted to write fiction or be an editor.

To say I was naive would have been generous.

I began to feel the stress and anxiety that comes with college coursework and the social pressures of life on a small campus. My living situation was uncomfortable. The stuffy rooms and lack of air conditioning made sleeping difficult in the outdated dorm facilities in the humid summer months. This would have been bearable had I been succeeding in my academic endeavors. However, I was not. Classes were not going well. Turns out, college is hard; who would have thought?

I needed an escape.

After classes were done for the day, and not wanting to return to my sauna of a dorm, I would hop in my car and drive away from campus. As I was not native to the region, I found myself spending a lot of time simply driving around for no other reason than to find out what the county had to offer. Typically, my ritual was to grab my iPod, hit up a gas station, buy a few cheap cigars, pick a direction I had yet to traverse, and go, sometimes for twenty minutes, other times for hours. With the air condition on max of course. Every backroad, small town, or poorly maintained dirt road was an opportunity to see something new. Soon, I took notice of abandoned farmhouses, churches, business, and bridges—structures that once served a purposed, but have since been left to rot.

Their aesthetic appealed to my anxiety filled conscious. Whereas campus was filled with the constant pressure of academics, interpersonal obstacles, and the constant thought of making sure my tens-of-thousands of dollars were not going to waste, these places were resoundingly quiet, still, and nonjudgmental. I could breathe.

Before long, I had stumbled across dozens of abandoned homesteads, farmhouses, bridges, and rural churches simply by chance. The idea then occurred to me: I have a camera. I should document these places. Perhaps on a blog or a website.

So, I did.

I registered the username "Abandoned Iowa" on a blogging service in 2010. My format was simple: take a few pictures and write a reflection. Much to my surprise, people started to notice. Soon, I had a few dozen followers. After a couple months, a few hundred.

After weeks of post-class outings and weekend adventures to nearby rural communities, I migrated my page and photos to Facebook. I quickly amassed thousands of "likes." My college coursework was lagging, but my new-found hobby was rapidly flourishing.

My process remained the same for years: go somewhere unfamiliar and take a camera. Document what I saw. Research the structures and write a reflection.

I initially enrolled as an English major because I wanted to write. Turns out, you don't need a degree to do that. During my second year of classes, I switched my major and academic direction to a more personally fulfilling path, environmental science. After abandoning the English major and picking up the sciences, I came to an ironic conclusion. I began to achieve what I initially set out to do in college: write! Abandoned Iowa WAS writing. It was creative, fulfilling, adventurous, and original writing.

In summer of 2013, I graduated. Despite my initial failure to launch, I earned a bachelor's degree. The diploma was in my hands; I was done.

But Abandoned Iowa was not.

Despite moving back to my hometown, the urge to seek out abandoned structures persisted. This often meant driving longer distances to escape the familiarity of the region. But the trips were still fruitful. Eventually I became skilled at digging through online public records, county assessor's information, and satellite imagery to find my subjects.

As the amount of content increased, so too did my online presence. I reached 5,000 followers, 10,000, 15,000. Each post garnered more attention. Viewers would comment with their own memories of the places I documented. I started to see that, although I began this project for me and my own creative purposes, people had an emotional stake in these places. Thus, a new driving force started to push me to consistently produce new content.

A question that is frequently asked is: how do I find abandoned structures? The answer is multifaceted. To start, I'll pull up satellite imagery of an area I simply have not been before. Google Maps is invaluable at giving me visual clues that may indicate an abandoned structure, dilapidated bridge, or crumbling school. In overhead views, I look for cracked and overgrown parking lots. The green, webbed pattern of grass and weeds contrasts to the gray concrete. Other times, looking at rooftops of large buildings in satellite images reveals collapsed beams and caved-in ceilings. If I find myself bored on a free afternoon, or simply feel the need to get out of the house, I'll jump in my car and hit the road.

When I started the project, I was in college in Marion County, a region I had not spent much time. With this unfamiliarity came opportunity. Once I had the idea of "Abandoned Iowa" and knew what I wanted to capture, the adventure began. I simply drove into the countryside, many times without direction or a notion of where I wanted to go. Gravel roads, level-b dirt roads, anything that was open to the public, I explored. From there, I developed a strategy.

After multiple trips to the same areas and feeling as though I had seen everything I could in my current geographic area, I would pick a city. That city became my destination. Each small town and dirt road between my current place of residence and that target, became my territory. Systematically, I drove across the Iowa countryside. Thankfully, due to farming and land practices, much of the central Iowan countryside is conveniently divided into square tracts of land. I scoured hundreds and hundreds of miles of dirt and gravel roads, seeking structures that thematically contributed to the vision of Abandoned Iowa. Internally, this process of simply hitting the road without a specific location in my mind became known as "freestyling."

Freestyling is how I discovered many of the structures in my pictures. There simply is not a database where abandoned structures are documented. No "condemned compendium" exists. It was up to my own sense of adventure and rural navigation to re-discover these lost, often forgotten, locations.

Although freestyling led to dozens of discoveries, I will resort to more precise methods. When aiming for a distant city or more targeted destination, I affectionately use the term "going deep," deep describing a region or city well out of my day-to-day geographic area.

The itch to get out, explore, and shoot photos comes and goes. Sometimes it comes between paychecks or at times when my wallet would rather be opened at a local grocery store than a gas station some hundred miles away from home. In these situations, or if I'm simply in the mood for a road trip, I'll open a map (yes, a paper map), pick a city I have not visited outside my typical stomping grounds, and make a day of it. Sometimes I'll stop along the way if a convenient photographic opportunity presents itself.

Whether I'm "going deep" or "freestyling," I will often seek geographical or natural clues that lead to abandonments. For example, due to the small number of native

Iowan evergreens, the presence of pines might indicate a previously inhabited area where the trees were intentionally planted. A long line of unkept evergreens might be a former windbreak or designate a perimeter of a now-deserted gravel driveway to a once-thriving farmstead. Large groves of young deciduous trees might conceal a former school or church.

Human-made clues such as crooked powerlines, crumbling grain silos, or dead-end signs often lead to abandoned discoveries as well. Often, powerline poles will remain standing long after their lines have been removed.

Humanity's need for water makes large creeks and rivers targets of exploration. Entire towns have been removed from existence due to flooding or the creation of reservoirs, as evident from the remnants of train tracks, highways, and bridges now only viewable during low-water conditions at Lake Red Rock.

In periods of low water levels at Lake Red Rock, remnants of the previous Highway 14 can be seen resting in the shallows.

Train tracks and timbers cross the remains of Highway 14 in Lake Red Rock.

1

BRIDGES

I owa's rural communities have long been connected via rural highways, gravel roads, and steel-framed bridges—often the only means of connection to civilization. Rural bridges are highly photogenic and easily accessed, making them excellent subjects for abandoned and rural exploration photography.

Iowa River E. Avenue Bridge

Built in 1938, the E Avenue Bridge crosses the Iowa River to the east of the small town of Montour. The western approach has been severely eroded. All access to the bridge has been cut off, and its massive frame and solid deck are now left to the elements, as with so many similar trusses around Iowa's countryside.

The eroded western approach of the E. Iowa Street Bridge near Montour.

A view of the super-structure of the E. Iowa Street Bridge.

The eastern approach.

BERWICK RAILROAD BRIDGE

Many bridges find new life for pedestrians and bicyclists. Iowa's once extensive railroad network crisscrossed the countryside. Many bridges and trusses that once used to carry trains across streams and rivers have been refurbished and integrated into existing and newly constructed bike trails.

The Chichaqua Valley Trail near Berwick hosts another rail-to-trail bridge. The steel and wooden structure once carried trains along the Chicago Great Western Rail line. Now, it is revitalized and reinforced for recreational use.

Above: Rails have long been removed on the train bridge near Berwick.

Opposite above: A view of the bridge prior to its renovation.

Opposite below: A look at the underside.

CGW - Raccoon River Trestle

Much like the trestle in Berwick, the Chicago Great Western Rail Line used to travel this bridge over the middle branch of the Raccoon River outside of the town of Carroll. The Sauk Rail Trail bike path runs underneath the train trestle, taking pedestrians and bicyclists through the shadow of the rail line. It is unknown at this time if the bridge will be renovated for trail use in the future or if it shall simply remain as it is. Now, the rails and timbers have been removed, leaving only remnants of the rail bed and the trestle as reminders of the former CGW Rail Line.

The former rail bridge crosses over a local bike trail near Carroll.

Above left: Rails were once spiked into place on the deck.

Above right: A look at the sturdy beams and hardware used in the construction of the bridge.

ADEL BRIDGE

At the site of a river ferry established just three years after the town of Adel was established remains the nearly 400-foot-long Adel Bridge. Built in 1882, the double-span bridge immediately became important to the community and travelers through the town. It served as the primary entry into the town and was part of the Historic US Route 6 highway—the longest in America at one time. The Adel Bridge carried regular traffic until 1932, when another nearby highway bridge was constructed. The bridge continued to serve vehicle traffic until its closure in 2000. Due to its historical status, unique design, and its current intact state, the Adel Bridge was added to the National Register of Historic Places in 2002.

The Adel Bridge on a chilly winter morning.

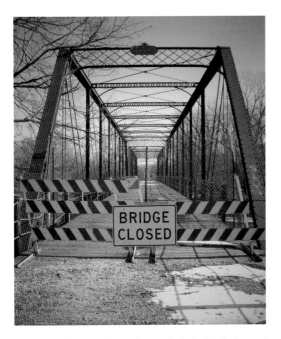

Above left: The portal bears the mark of the fabricator and manufacturer.

Modern footings, and a river-level gauge, were added later in the bridge's life.

BELLE FOUNTAIN BRIDGE

At 600 ft. long, the lengthy remains of the Belle Fountain Bridge can be found just east of the small town of Tracy. Constructed in 1898, the bridge replaced a ferry in the former town of Belle Fountain. The bridge at one time carried traffic from Ashland Avenue over the Des Moines River. Notable for having three distinct spans, the Belle Fountain Bridge began to be neglected following construction of the Old Highway 92 bridge a half-mile upstream in 1930. The bridge has since been left unmaintained, with its deck nearly nonexistent and portals overgrown with trees and vines. In 1998, the Belle Fountain Bridge was added to the National Register of Historic Places.

Only a few boards remain on the deck of the Bellefontaine Bridge.

Above: An ornate light fixture
reaches off the bridge.

Hard to fit the massive four-span bridge into frame.

Looking upstream.

EVELAND BRIDGE

Only a few miles downstream of the Belle Fountain Bridge sits the Eveland Bridge. Like its partner upstream, this bridge was built at a former ferry site. Constructed in 1877, the Eveland Bridge, or Wilson's Ferry Bridge to some, is one of the oldest remaining bridges on the Des Moines River. The bridge underwent reconstruction and rebuilding in the early 1900s following damage from a flood. Operating a regular crossing of traffic for nearly ninety years, Eveland Bridge was closed to all traffic in the 1990s and currently sits in a state of neglect. The deck has completely eroded away with only a few random boards scattered about.

The Northern portal of the Eveland Bridge is entirely overgrown during the spring and summer months.

Ice still chips away at the stone and concrete footings.

VALLEYVIEW BRIDGE

Residing on its namesake stretch of dirt road in western Madison County, the Valleyview Bridge was a humble, unassuming, single-span bridge unlike the multiple hundred-feet-long cousins Eveland and Belle Fountain. Built in 1911, the Valleyview Bridge served as a crossing over the Middle River for decades. Unfortunately, multiple flood events took their toll on the bridge portals. The southern approach was completely eroded away, leaving only a massive diving board-like section of the bridge precariously dangling over the sandy banks of the river.

The Valleyview Bridge was not destined for the scrapyard, despite its state at the time these photos were taken. With the help of county engineers, the bridge has successfully been relocated to serve as a crossing for pedestrians and bicyclists over the spillway at Cedar Lake in Winterset, Iowa.

The Southern portal of the Valleyview Bridge.

A look at the mostly intact bridge deck.

Below: Water erosion from flooding washed away the soil under the northern approach.

KATE SHELLEY HIGH BRIDGE

Kate Shelley was a Midwestern Iowan woman who happened to make history one night during a tempestuous thunderstorm. Shelley sat at home on the evening of June 6, 1881, when an inspection locomotive carrying four men crashed into a local creek following its destruction due to heavy rains. She heard the crash. Knowing a loaded passenger train was set to take the same route around midnight, Shelley acted. Lives were at stake, including her own, as she crossed the Des Moines River via the Moingona Bridge on her hands and knees after her lantern blew out during the thunderstorm. Shelley traveled for miles to get to the Moingona Train Depot to sound an alarm and warn the oncoming passenger train of the washout. Her actions saved the lives of two of the inspectors from the wrecked locomotive still trapped in the swollen creek and potentially hundreds more on the passenger train. Shelley was heralded a hero for her bravery. Her legacy lives on. A historic railroad viaduct standing 200 feet over the Des Moines River bears her name.

Perhaps the most famous of Iowan bridges, the Kate Shelley High Bridge—or the Boone Viaduct officially—was built in 1901 to carry passenger and freight trains. It stretches a half-mile over the Des Moines River Valley. According to Report of the Historic American Engineering Record, "The bridge was the longest and heaviest viaduct of its time and may be the longest extant double-track railroad viaduct in the world."

To clarify, this bridge was not crossed by its namesake Kate Shelly during the fateful night in 1881 that solidified her as a local hero. In fact, multiple bridges have been christened the "Kate Shelly Bridge" at one point. A small stone bridge near Shelley's home is also often referred to as the "Kate Shelly Bridge." However, it was the multiple-span steel bridge in the town of Moingona that was, in fact, the famous bridge Shelley crossed on the night of the locomotive crash.

The Kate Shelley High Bridge remained in use by railroads until the completion of a more modern, longer, concrete and steel bridge parallel to the existing steel bridge in 2009. Due to its length, local history, and namesake, the Boone Viaduct was added to the National Register of Historic Places in 1978.

A view of the dirt road approaching the Kate Shelly High Bridge

The modern concrete bridge runs parallel to the former previous Kate Shelly High Bridge over the Des Moines River.

WAGON WHEEL BRIDGE

Upstream from the Kate Shelley High Bridge once stood a significant piece of Iowan history. The Wagon Wheel Bridge stretched over 700 feet across the Des Moines River. Four spans representing two distinctive truss styles imbued the bridge with a distinctive style and unique quality unmatched by other Des Moines River crossings. Its construction and design were unique when it was erected in 1909. The Wagon Wheel Bridge was added to the National Register of Historic Places in 1998. Its four spans remained open to traffic until its closure due to damage from the devastating 2008 floods.

Sadly, the Wagon Wheel Bridge met its demise in winter of 2015. An ice jam in February of 2015 caused significant damage to a vital support, causing a center span to twist and contort downstream. A short time later in March, the span crumbled into the river below, causing significant damage to the connecting spans. Renovation and repair would be near impossible. The Wagon Wheel Bridge was to be demolished following a century of service to the surrounding communities. The remaining spans were removed in their entirety that following June.

The ice-covered Des Moines River foreshadows the Wagon Wheel Bridge's demise.

Looking from west to the east.

2

SCHOOLS

I n the early twentieth century, one-room schoolhouses and rural communities began to consolidate their districts and students into larger buildings. This consolidation process brought students and residents from the surrounding rural areas together under one roof. Typically, kindergarten through twelfth grade was taught in the same building.

However, many of these small communities began to shrink. Residents moved away from the agricultural-based livelihoods for more abundant and fruitful work in larger, more developed urban areas. The class size began to dwindle. Soon, many of the large consolidated school buildings, which once hosted students of all ages, began to focus on elementary-age children. Middle and high school students were once again consolidated to larger school districts.

From the 60s onward, many of the massive brick and mortar schools in the smaller communities began to close. Their doors boarded up, windows were removed, and the structures were left to the will of the elements. Some were converted to apartments or community centers. Others found no such afterlife and became abandoned.

Governor Terry Branstad once pushed for a tax credit to restore and refurbish some of the former consolidated schools:

> Yet, some of the schools and public buildings which used to be the source of that pride are now empty shells dotting the landscapes of our communities. Once filled with the hustle and bustle of schoolchildren and their teachers, these are more than just abandoned buildings. They hold a part of our childhood. They hold a part of us.
>
> Instead of letting these treasures stand empty, let's turn them into the economic centers of our communities. Let's once again make them part of our daily lives. We will submit legislation to provide tax incentives to repurpose abandoned schools and public buildings.

While this initiative was comforting for many residents of the towns where former school buildings exist, it simply was not and is not economically nor architecturally viable in most situations. Many of the buildings presented in this book still contain asbestos and lead paint, substances that require costly remediation and removal processes.

Keep in mind that many of these schools were built before the Americans with Disabilities Act as well, making remediation and renovation more costly. Many of these buildings do not have ground-level entrances, or the capability to have elevators installed, for example.

Many of these schools remain standing not out of affection for the past, but rather the logistic and financial commitment that would be required for demolition.

A lone desk sits in the overgrowth next to the former school.

GARDINER CONSOLIDATED SCHOOL

The first students entered Gardiner Consolidated School nearly a century ago in 1920. First through tenth grade classes were taught in this rural building near the town of small town of Perry. The final class of eighth graders graduated from Gardiner Consolidated in 1958. Nature has since reclaimed the building following the sale of the land in 1964.

A door frame stands amidst the collapsed floors of the school.

Above: A farmer's field surrounds the school lot.

Left: Weeds and grass consume the stairs once leading to the front grounds of the school.

A dense grove of trees once surrounded the school building.

The masonry sign peaks through the foliage.

A dark doorway where children once lined up for the day's lessons.

Nearly every floor in the school has collapsed into a heap.

A former classroom. One of the only intact floors left in the school.

Above: Crumbling brick and mortar litter the former grounds of the school.

Left: Sun peeking through a darkened doorway.

Right: Plaster peeling away from the walls.

Left: A second-floor landing.

SEARSBORO CONSOLIDATED SCHOOL

The grand structure of Searsboro Consolidated school was erected in 1936. With hallways and stairs made from marble, the school is unique in its scale and aesthetic—especially when contrasted with the now-unincorporated town of Searsboro. Eventually, the Searsboro School district consolidated with the Lynnville-Sully district and the building ceased to be a place of education. The small town is beginning to resemble the school itself: exposed to the elements, overgrown, and slowly withering away.

The massive three-story Searsboro Consolidated School.

Shattered ornate glass blocks.

A shadowy entrance into the ruins of the school.

Right: Little indication remains of the school's classrooms.

Left: Plaster chips and peels away from the brick amid shards of porcelain bathroom fixtures.

LUTHER CONSOLIDATED SCHOOL

Along Iowa Highway 17, not far from the town of Boone, sits the small town of Luther, a quaint rural Iowan town with a present population of just over 100 residents. Luther, however, was once lively and thrived with local agricultural business and industry. In 1916, Luther Consolidated School opened its doors to approximately 200 kindergarten through twelfth grade students. The school served Luther and the rural residents of the surrounding countryside. Many students passed through its doors until consolidating with the neighboring Napier and Jordan schools to form the United Community School District in 1957.

The Luther Consolidated School building then served as an elementary school until its closure in 1972. The building remained standing, albeit unmaintained, for decades after. The windows were removed, the doors boarded, and the only students attending classes were flocks of birds and raccoons. The building was finally torn down in 2015, following the purchase of the land by a local business over.

Attempts were made to secure the building from human intruders.

Above: The stone-work school nameplate.

Left: The fire escape remains fixed to the building.

MONTOUR CONSOLIDATED SCHOOL

The Montour Consolidated School was constructed in 1936 to replace the one-roomed school that once occupied the site. The school served kindergarten through twelfth grade for decades. Middle and high school students were subsequently transferred to other districts. Class sizes began to diminish in the 70s onward. By the 1980s, only 100 students between kindergarten and fifth grade attended classes. The building continued to serve as an elementary school until its closure in 2001. Less than forty students total attended class in its final year of operation.

The bright blue door contrasts with the rest of the deep red-brick structure of Montour School.

Shadows and light create an abstract scene in the basement of the school.

The posterior side of the Montour School.

BAGLEY SCHOOL

Guthrie County is home to a number of small towns with diminishing populations. Bagley, home to roughly 300, residents is no different. The former Bagley School building itself has resembled the town for years. The roof of the three-story structure collapsed years ago following a blizzard. The building has since become an eyesore for the locals. More of building caves in with each passing season. The fire escape slide remains fixed to the building, clinging desperately to the brick structure as beams and blocks crumble around it. An addition was built at some point which served as a kindergarten and elementary school. The addition was made into a private residence by a local buyer. Demolition will be costly, and with the city of Bagley facing a shrinking population and a severe water quality issue, the school will more likely remain standing until nature finishes it off.

GENESEO SCHOOL

Geneseo school was built in 1921. Like other consolidated schools of its kind, classes of kindergarteners through twelfth grade students attended for decades. Over 540 diplomas were handed out to graduating seniors before merging with the Dysart school district in the late 60s. Despite the school's construction of an additional wing, Geneseo fell victim to declining enrollment. The school closed its doors, and in the early 80s, the property was sold, and its contents auctioned off. Today, the school remains standing, overshadowing an active church just yards from the doors through which hundreds of students once passed.

Two brick pillars still stand at the entrance to the Bagley school grounds.

Note the collapsed wall and non-existent roof.

The tightly boarded-up structure of Geneseo School.

Windows from a former classroom look out over the former grounds of the school.

A gymnasium and auditorium overgrown with saplings and weeds.

The rusted basketball hoop still fastened to the wall of the gymnasium.

Above left: A solitary curtain dangles from the loft of the stage.

Above right: Ropes hang from the ceiling of the stage.

CARROLLTON SCHOOL

Located in Carroll County, not far from the city of Carroll, this school building was the only remnant of the former town of Carrollton. The building and land were under private ownership for many years. The yard where children once assembled for classes was turned into a makeshift junkyard. The school was demolished five years ago. A park containing a small memorial and information on the former town has since been erected in a nearby lot.

The hollowed structure of Carrollton School.

The tarnished door fixtures fixed to the front entrance of the school.

ONE-ROOM SCHOOLHOUSE

The cackling fire in the belly of the stove filled the small classroom of the country schoolhouse with the scent of charred wood. Farm children from the local area dragged their limestone chalk across the blackboards at the front of the class where the vigilant teacher kept their watchful eye open for penmanship errors. Lambskin rags were used to erase the slate panels used by students for everything from arithmetic to grammar and punctuation practice.

Boys and girls were expected to help maintain and clean the schoolhouse itself. Maybe an older child would fetch water from an on-site well for the class to share while another student would bring in more wood for the stove.

Now, the stove no longer smolders. The dust from the limestone chalk has long since settled, and the blackboards have warped and cracked from being exposed to decades of weather. The schoolyard where students may have played or ran is indiscernible from the abundance of weeds and thistles that have taken over the remnants of the school grounds.

The quaint schoolhouse bordered by agricultural fields.

DINSDALE SCHOOL

The Dinsdale School was once a central pillar of the small community of the same name. The doors first opened to students in 1921, and like many consolidated schools, elementary to high school students were all taught under the same roof. Nearly 400 students graduated from Dinsdale during its forty-two-year lifespan. The school was closed, shuttered, and left to rot following its closure and subsequent abandonment in 1963.

The front steps of Dinsdale School surrounded by briars.

Original windows remain intact above the entrance to the school.

Above left: Almost all floors have collapsed into the basement.

Above right: Steps filled with powdered plaster and debris from the dilapidated school.

A window and doorway into a small office.

A blackboard still visibly clings to the wall amidst the crumbling floor.

3

MAIN STREET

A cross the state, the main streets through the town centers are drying up. Growing costs of living, prices of goods, and even the impact of internet commerce are all felt in these once-thriving communities.

Small towns and rural communities which were once home to "mom and pop" restaurants now resemble ghost towns. The main drags are spotted with bars and a few shops or eateries here and there, but are hardly at maximum occupancy.

A now shuttered post office.

The remains of a vacant café.

Above: Vacant storefronts line the main streets of small towns across Iowa.

Right: Small grocery stores, butchers, and bakers were once common across the state.

PEORIA GAS AND FEED

This old feed and farm supply store is the only remnant of any sort of commercial development in this town of less than a few hundred people. Old gasoline and kerosene fuel pumps were still firmly planted in the concrete parking area. The doors and windows were all boarded up.

General stores sold everything rural families and their livestock may have needed.

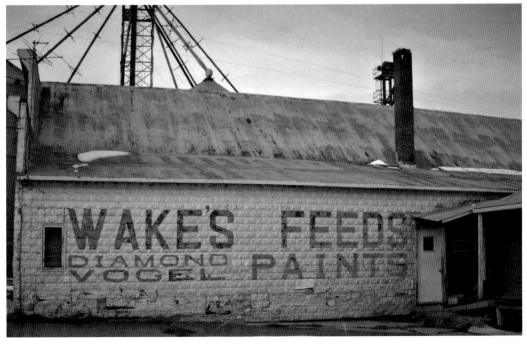

THAYER POST OFFICE

A vacant post office sits in the center of the town of Thayer. The tiny town of Thayer is home to under sixty residents and has been unincorporated for many years.

The darkened structure of a former post office.

New Sharon Purina

If you happen to visit the south-east side of the small town of New Sharon, then you have inescapably noticed this monolith of a grain elevator. Constructed entirely out of concrete, this massive spire of an elevator once dispensed feed grains onto farm trucks and rail cars. The Purina logo is just faintly visible near the crown of this monument to a different era.

The concrete monolith towers over the small community.

MINBURN CAFÉ

"What'll it be hon?"

"How 'bout a warm cup of mildew, and a plate of black mold with mildew over easy?"

This quaint cafe rests in the small town of Minburn. Windows boarded and roof buckling, the last patron has long since dined.

Order up.

Once warm and inviting, this café has long since closed its doors to patrons.

4

CHURCHES

For centuries, churches served not only as a place of worship and spiritual reflection, but community centers—places for residents to gather, exchange pleasantries, catch up with friends and family, and perhaps share a meal after the services. Rural churches were places for the baptisms of the newborn, and the final Earthly destinations of the previous generations.

But, as populations decline, and the number of non-religious grows, these sacred places will inevitably shut their doors. Shrinking congregations leads to less money in the donation tray. Less donations leads to cutbacks and closures.

Even holy centers cannot escape the inevitability of abandonment.

Memento, homo, quia pulvis es, et in pulverem reverteris.

LOUCKS GROVE CHURCH

Residing in the rural Adair County countryside near the town of Greenfield sits Loucks Grove Church. The doors of the church first opened and welcomed its congregation almost 125 years ago. Its current state is a historic example of Gothic architecture, being the only Gothic-style church remaining in Adair County. The arched windows and doorways exhibit the original Gothic design. The church remains unchanged—sans upgraded electrical and heating systems—from its original construction in 1895. All but one of the pine pews which formerly lined the sanctuary have been removed. The church was added to the National Register of Historic Places in 1995.

Above: A view of the church from the neighboring cemetery.

Left: The doorway where parishioners entered for prayers and worship.

Above: Paint peels and flakes from the church ceiling.

Left: Light filters in through the entryway and an empty window frame.

Above: A piano still stands in the sanctuary; its last hymn has long since played.

Right: Dated electrical components dangle from the ceiling.

Note the Gothic-style windows.

AFTON PRESBYTERIAN CHURCH

Anyone who has experienced an Iowa spring and summer has inevitably experienced the ferocity of a thunderstorm. Punishing winds sweep across the plains and corn fields. The former Presbyterian Church in Afton unfortunately was unable to withstand the power of an unusually strong storm in June of 2018.

While already abandoned, and its congregation long relocated, the church was boarded and sealed for decades until the intense storm blew out the remaining stained-glass windows. The church was irreparably damaged and has since been demolished. Now, only a vacant lot remains. Stray bricks on its former foundation are the only reminders of its existence.

The bell tower on the corner of the church.

Entrances and windows shuttered and boarded.

EVANGELICAL UNITED BRETHREN CHURCH

Build in the late 1800s, Evangelical United Brethren Church served the small community of Ackley for decades. The EUB merged with the Methodist Church in the late 60s. A United Methodist Church was constructed a short distance away, resulting in the closure of the former EUB Church. The building was sold to private owners, who operated an antique shop out of it for many years. Ultimately, the shop closed and the building became a glorified storage shed. Currently, the church remains in poor condition, overgrown with vines and brambles. Little evidence of its former life remains, *sans* the ornate stained-glass windows.

The entrance to the former church overgrown by vines and ivy.

Stained glass being consumed by growth.

5

HOMESTEADS

The state of Iowa often frequently copes with the changing cycles of nature, dry and wet seasons and periods of growth and of dormancy. The American economy exhibits similar traits. During the early and mid-seventies, the economy of the United States was relatively healthy.

Following the "go big or go home" attitude promoted by the Nixon administration's Secretary of Agriculture Earl Butz, many smaller farms were forced to compete with the new "fence row to fence row" style of farming that boomed in the mid-twentieth century, and many, sometimes through lack of money or lack of labor, shriveled up and caved into ambitious land buyers. Abandoned farmhouses, barns, silos, and outbuildings became a common sight across the Iowa countryside.

Interest rates were low, which in Iowa meant farmers could borrow money cheaply and at little risk. However, during the late seventies, the economy began winding down; a downturn in production caused interest rates to skyrocket, a bad omen for farmers who relied on loans to purchase equipment and land.

The shrinking economy caused a ripple effect in commodities markets as well; consumers were simply not spending as much money across the board. Commodity prices took another hit after the Russian invasion of Afghanistan in January of 1980 occurred. President Jimmy Carter protested the occupation of Afghanistan and military campaigns of Russia by placing a trade embargo on grain sales to Afghanistan, which crippled the foreign markets for American-produced grain and corn. In April of 1980, President Carter publicly announced the state of the economy as being in a recession after inflation reached nearly ten percent and interest rates climbed upwards to eighteen to twenty percent.

A long-abandoned farmstead on a cool autumn day.

A hollowed house sits beyond a barbed-wire fence.

Left: The rusty cross posts of a long-forgotten clothesline.

Below: A grasshopper clings to a weathered clothespin.

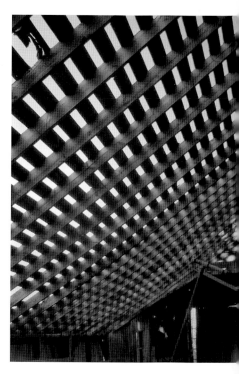

Above left: A distinctively arched barn.

Above right: Light filters through the slats of a now uncovered barn roof.

A vintage Pontiac sits on the grounds of an overgrown homestead.

With less demand for their products, and lower commodity prices, farmers across the Midwest became burdened with insurmountable debt. Many would simply take out more loans in hopes that the economy would turn around in the coming years.

Farmers lost their homes, land, and their livelihood. Family farms dried up; only the wealthiest of landowners were able to keep their operations afloat. Foreclosed land and implement auctions became commonplace, with many farmers simply trying to sell anything they could to generate some sort of income. It was during this period that many of these wealthier landowners were able to buy up several hundred to 1,000 acres of land at a time, which led to a decrease in the number of farmers overall, but an increase in acres farmed nationwide.

This led to a ripple effect that can still be felt today and that is the start of the sharp decrease in young, start-up farmers. Farming simply wasn't profitable, and without some sort of incentive, it was largely avoided as an occupation. This change created a sort of exodus of the younger generation from rural communities to where more jobs could be found, primarily in bigger cities.

Vintage Iowa.